FREE STREAM VELOCITY

John Olson

BLACK SQUARE EDITIONS
New York, NY

Acknowledgments
I am grateful to the editors of the following publications in which
some of these prose poems first appeared: *Bird Dog, First Intensity,
hemorrhagingimaging, unarmed, Untitled.*

ISBN 0-9744065-0-3

Cover art by Thomas Nozkowski
UNTITLED (W-65), 1992
pencil, colored pencil
and ballpoint pen on paper
9" x 12"
Courtesy of Max Protetch Gallery, New York

Book and cover design: Lee Chapman

Distributed by
Small Press Distribution
1341 Seventh St.
Berkeley, CA 94710-1409

Published by
Black Square Editions
1200 Broadway, Suite 3-C
New York, NY 10001

For Roberta

CONTENTS

NOW THAT THE SUN HAS RISEN

NOW THAT the sun has risen it converts everything to mustard. It shines natural as a membrane. Whatever a human being thinks, science is riddled with riddles. But the sun is a sun and the splendid fallen leaves reveal nary a strawberry. Let this leopard leap through its demonstrations and serve as an oboe for the phenomena of bats. All the king's horses are empirical and all the annals are green. He who sloshes around in manure knows how superb the thread of existence holding the price of fish together in its travel. The atmosphere is coined into words. Each word displays the visible struggle of meaning. Facts are fruit. Every apple, every lemon, every cherry precipitates X-rays of itself among the Poets of Investigation. Science is green. It sees coconuts on television where others see pipes and eloquent liquids. Facts of ermine drool fat and furry humps in the realm of the bacillus. The medicine cabinet bleeds images of California. The gargoyles consist of granite and marble and their muscles describe outbursts of cellular growth frozen forever in a snowshoe. The candidates are dripping with optimism, but the pessimists celebrate obsidian. It is the peculiarity of softness to make life more tolerable than it is, to help usher us into the spotlights of trophoblastic pink and remember our monologues alone in the rain. Most stories begin at the beginning, like the metaphysics of grapes, but the mutuality of our horticulture belongs to the relics of heaven, and stand outside of time, like exertion and garlic. Science maps our way. Here in the House of Decorum the language of our thighs demonstrates relation among our knees, thimbles among our thumbs. Distant examples of light rim the Ferrari

in the garage, or just outside of the garage, where it has been
freshly hosed. It bears nothing similar to a Brazilian river but
the scientific epoxy of imminent catastrophe. The zipper was
invented in a rotunda. We know this because life is absor-
bent, its puddles abandoned and hammered into water by an
iron giant called winter. The stars are mammoths, sing the
geese, and travel requires soap. Method flaps with encore in
a field of sperm, every plateau reflecting the method of the
clouds, which have no method, but the method of floating,
the method of drifting over the cattle too big to wear garters,
too misty to care. They are sumptous facts of buoyant coral,
great illuminations churning with valentines and Jurassic
chandeliers, those giant acacias fanning overhead in our
dreams of Indiana. Sequence comes in gallons, not in levers.
Narrative is digestive and metabolic. It is our organs that
ooze soliloquies and color our experience with balloons and
carpets. Our road is strewn with panties, each one convulsive
as the present tense of a cloud of spawning salmon. The
watermelon completes the cage of itself when the solid glints
of a ghostly dog of extreme diversion reveals a man applying
for a job as a legacy. Science slides through our glands trying
to make sense of ourselves as roots and drugs, humming
wires social as cloth. If method tastes of vanilla, it is because
the jacket we wear is constructed of the lumber of heaven,
and sports a breastpocket on which a pharaonic worm has
been sewn like a mystical statistic percolating Egypt. There is
a method for putting on a brassiere and a method for taking
it off. Each scientific scheme is fat and renewable and
occupies the wildest library imaginable. I know a woman
who really likes London and classifies goats as explosions. I
know a man with an artificial personality and a girl with a
flute of Spanish silver spurting rubies and thorns. Habit is a

crisp classification of the throat whose chords extend for 140 miles. The best way to overcome a mind full of fish is to go fishing. Science heaves with hydropower, fueling an industry of aromatic problems and cities of speech. If a man enters the casino insinuating blues and bleeding syllables of steaming proficiency, let him play blackjack rippling with poplars and tractors, a plate of squid beneath his ceaseless vibrato. I once saw a group of scientists standing in a bog holding a set of ancient tweezers when almost any common ladle would do. If the mind goes in circles, give it raw violins. The unity of iron reveals, at times, a kind of paint. But it takes much more than a ratio or a museum to make a heron enter a tunnel of rainwater in a dark Brazil of shameless fiction. I've dealt with this kind of cartilage before. A fugitive hue of mechanical black indicates life is a wound of existence on a great big train of crashing conviction. When it pulls through Malta everyone gazes at the water tower. A man lifts a spoon. A woman sips a glass of water. The train stops briefly, then goes on its way. I know of no other parable than this: when the hour of the hammer is clutching your shirt, drop your ratchet at the journey's end, and begin another, packing horseshoes and doorbells, and a bar of blue soap.

PHENOMENOLOGY OF HUNGER

IMAGINE A drapery opened for the first time, the view out the window, the smoking meat of a maniacal spider embroidered with morning, the many streams and diagonals, the curious soliloquies of the trees.

Imagine milk and laundry. A clam chiseled out of the ambiguity of gray. The Cartesian charm of a pancake, or an alley in Moscow. Glints of industry in a silver vagina wheeled around on a cart of tulips and glass.

Imagine yourself emerging into consciousness for the first time, your mind completely empty of all knowledge, all memory, all forms of measure and language. Everywhere you look the virtue of freight and the freight of virtue is multiplied by the voluptuous odor of cheddar. Hot silk circulating in a book. Sermons in stones. Gavels in gravel. Momentum in milk.

How might one imagine what it is to imagine? How might one imagine oneself imagining what it is to imagine oneself imagining oneself? How might one imagine oneself covered in scales or fur? How might one imagine spiritual intelligences which can warn us and advise us, circles in a Maori ceremony, the behavior of flutes, streams sparkling over colossal rocks, scraggly trees and casseroles of vigorous purposelessness?

Let us wander the landscape of the imagination. Here there are limes in a refrigerator of the mind, meat singing of the phenomenology of hunger, the charm of cabbage and the candor of food. The positive existence of mind is nothing but the immediate aspect of mind, observed Hegel. Hegel is a nice cool freezer in which we can dip our hands to collect bon bons, chunks of frost brushing our hands as we reach for that box on the bottom, the one with all the ideas in it, ideas of bone and poplar, ideas of the experiences through which consciousness passes, and the rapture of shape.

The door of the vault is creaking open: we see an enunciation prepare to pronounce itself. Eyes perched high on stalks allow ghostly crabs to watch for predators. Short thick prepositions appear like images taking shape in a darkroom, tingling examples of being representing space as a motel in North Dakota, sounds and smells rubbing against the air and returning to our lips in the form of speech, an engine of thought plunged in sorcery.

Who or what is responsible for creating the universe? Here is an Aztec square touched by the sun. Here is a cave of wonders, or the dreamy Fergus pondering a blade of Irish steel. We must excite our whole being into activity with roots and magnets. This is a ring of ripples. This is the cartilage of a turtle crawling in the sand and this is a reflection of the mind disturbed by dropping a stone in a Cartesian well. If the mind can exist without a body then how does it clutch experience? Experience is not a thing like a balloon but a citrus of the lips, an event bleeding architecture and fish, a word that is thick in the mouth, like the duration of mustard.

The inherent strangeness of being alive unwinds in lyric fluctuation, hydropower and shards of Ice Age orchid. The sap of divinity informs our veins and lungs. There is tungsten on the tongue and pizza in the oven. What is death? What is it to non-exist, as if to non-exist were a form of existence, a being that cannot be seen but sees, because non-existence is so very previous, so very hoarse and unscientific. Palpable as a hand. Merciful as mud.

A leatherback turtle lays her eggs at midnight and the world is made whole again. But what of the forms swelling into life as the brush of struggle is dipped in morning? When I say garter I mean something different from a thinly disguised membrane of pipes and eloquent liquids. I refer to an object that stretches, that demonstrates elasticity, that occurs to form a horse of decoration, a band of happy support around the leg. It is a symptom of free will, blinking colors enhanced by glass. Free will is a wonderful thing, like the X-ray of a vowel revealing smears of existence.

If one has free will, what does it mean to imagine the waters of heaven or the iron of hell, a higher order of existence, as we travel into the Valley of the Dead, or a salmon entering a stream, a bottle of wind or America and its tissue torched into fibers of phantasmal vegetation, hot gallons of pure existence brewing prodigies of turquoise? Have we sufficient imagination to imagine such a being as Nefertiti blowing soothing breath on a burned thumb, or the mud of Sumer receiving the impressions of a stylus, poplars around a farmhouse or a lion in the zoo riding a bicycle of glass? Are there omens in tread, in thread, in ferns and stains? Does the sky gargle coils of rising air only to collapse into ladders at night? Who can appear or disappear at will? What depth of emotion is still perhaps lacking in me because Welsh is not my language, or the candy of the clouds do not slide out of my esophagus in thrills of ivory-hued consistency, or that sprays of kelp do not untie themselves in superabundant guano when the moon travels about in reverie? What whimsical facility do we require to butter that cloud with sunset? Because the intelligence creating the universe is also you going about in emotion and garlic, breasts swollen with milk, snowshoes on your feet and a wet snout pressed against your hand.

The sun is a gas. We know this. Tahiti is transfused with its warmth. Yet what of the definition of beauty, smoked fish and dirigibles, Buddhism and the clatter of Shanghai? How do we know that the nose is an organ of smell and not merely the grandiloquence of skin? What is an emotion? The body wants reverberation, the mind wants veneration. Neither is deckle-edged or refrigerated in knowledge, yet everything tends that way, Alcatraz engulfed in the fog, a cat like an envelope with eyes.

FOG DRIP

LADIES AND gentlemen, my head is swimming. Swimming, yes, swimming. Swimming vis-a-vis these strange, mysterious, enigmatic, bizarre realities, these valentines and vacuums, gyroscopes and carrots. Call me what you want, but I know a graham cracker from a dumpling. I run a string of cathouses in the valley. The place is full of hydropower and paradise. Truckloads of clouds, merchants of pleasure and apothecaries selling their liquid business to the dry and the dodecaphonic. I can't talk. It's too much. I need some cannoli. I need to empty my head. Have you ever noticed how mustard is a yellow breath screwed to a species of light? The consequent theoretical attitude consists in judging these things a posteriori and not a priori. Gas is equipped with volatility and moisture like the storm of emotion in an oyster at low tide. I wear a patch over one eye and a false mustache mingled with a mechanical lip of golden theories clashing with the bones of a muskrat. I have constructed a testosterone satellite and put it in orbit around a hot feminine cabbage. The cherry orchard is now mine. Let us go look out upon the terrain and not disregard everything right away. The Boston ferns and rocks, the grapes and cattle. Sometimes I put on some green whiskers and a text of seeds that opens into a windswept delphinium when my feathers turn public and mauve. The most beautiful estate in the whole world is this dog-eared fog I am wrapping in the arteries of a ghost of representational garlic. I have done so in the name of a negative prejudgment, for which I am sorry and rubber. Reality is often brought to mind by the shine of the cookware and a certain slant of light. Hold the calls: I am going to describe this sensation as a bikini. Yes, a bikini. This brassiere of sticks, this rocky epoxy, this cloth entering our perception particular as candy and secret as a feeling of dark soil in Nebraska. Yes, that's right, I'm here every night stapling balloons to the ceiling and sifting space through time and momentum. The epistemological principle of comprehending everything, of receiving everything, is a passionate conception, don't you think, like herding cattle across the Texas border into Arkansas or Kansas. Autumn is more than a matter of weather: it is also dead leaves and pumpkins, the personality of a piano chiseled out of ivory and hidden in the dark of uncertainty. We are all engaged in a world of experience, n'est-ce pas? Blueprint and bouillon, Nefertiti's heiroglyphic halls. I come here every night to ponder the iron eyes of death, the trophoblastic door and its junkyard paint. This is my job, this is what I do for a living. I come up here and I do the best I can. You call me up and tell me things about myself, how swollen and disturbed I am. Well, so what? We all have our blossoms, our trellis on the wall. Certain phenomena cannot be excluded from their historical reality. Structuralist cocoons opening into bells and chivalry, epic bananas and rubies and waterfalls. I'm just a voice, after all, a vertebrae of feverish opals inaccurately blue. Hey, musicians, play, I want to hear you. Come on everybody, let's scribble ourselves into existence. Let's use everything we have at our disposal: levitation, stigmata, the luminescence of bodies, fever, out of body experiences, living on air, the ability to endure pain. Music, strike up! These phenomena have been observed and detailed. I feel reality slipping into a nightgown. I feel a mushy dollop of beauty rubbing against my museum. Decades and levers, a voice in the wilderness fumbling a marvelous black hose.

Listen: you think I'm crazy about the warehouse? You think I'm in love with continental shoes? The admissability of witnessed testimonies, their authenticity, have been the object of serious work by competent historians who have only just arrived at the beginning of their journey. The sky is more than oxygen: the sky is also a regime of clouds and stars. Over the years there has been many a penis insinuated into the silk morning of some motel with percale sheets and fluorescent tubes. And so, from hour to hour, we ripe and ripe. And then, from hour to hour, we rot and rot. How lucky dead people are. They've already been through all that. What do you want to talk about? Joyrides and glands? Sure, why not. In so far as it manifests itself in phenomenality, a sitar might be imagined as a river of sound moving through the arteries and nerves of our attention. The strange currency of history is largely inflated with treasures of feeling buttered with autumn. That is to say, everything we catalogue is but the ardor of our odor, coliseums tickled into thought. Each experience has its intentional object which, accordingly, has a meaning. The hardware of poetry is submerged in calamity. Emotions are the cargo of a story whose Ferrari is upholstered with lime. Even the cartilage of structure mimics the garrulity of milk. I spin away fortunes on the roulette wheel and no one says a thing. Silk tells the vertebrae to relax. The camera grabs images out of the artifacts of existence and develops them into passports. And thereby hangs a tale.

IMMIGRANT IMMERSION

A CHIN FULL of seeds and a prelude full of humidity, Huey Woolbright dove into an aberration of narrative fabric and swam to the bottom of a lake looking for yesterday's wrench. He did not find the wrench but he did find a logarithmic valentine of mushy sentiment buttoned in horticultural trapezoids and a pair of boots that resembled cyclones of golden rubber. These items he collected and put in his basket of unwitting proteins.

He also discovered Berlin lying around on a colossal black clay of warm vitality, much like a vignette involving a dress code and a crowbar prefaced with gum, and a blend of various annals whose theories on wind and hay caused his pigments to turn into a village of vichysoisse and lightbulbs. Burlap, he thought, is not an opponent to aesthetical judgments but a type of fabric whose thatch and delphinium propose an engine of bluish white metallic elements. The sensations of colors and tones have a right to be regarded as burlap only in so far as they are burlap. Those things which do not belong to the complete representation of the object internally as elements, but only externally as complements, must also be considered burlap. Each strand holds a potential sack in its purposive purposelessness, which is the essential condition of a judgment about burlap. It is of the greatest importance in a critique of taste to decide whether burlap can thus actually be resolved into the concept of fabric. If not, it is perhaps best to look elsewhere.

It became obvious that Huey was stuck in a web of burlap, a wind of insinuated hair and iron filled with the violent blood of a ceiling of swords. He blew a conch shell and a blade of hemispheric unexpectedness appeared in a deity of bunting and allspice and gargled the winds sloshing around in his signature fins. He adjusted his bracelet of rocky initiative and clashing muskrats and tasted the citrus of fate as it bubbled up from a village of turgid forms and country dances. There was a lump in his throat whose bloodred cartilage vibrated like an astringent ratio. This was not a good sign. His breath would smell like a theatre for days.

He looked at his watch. The judgment of taste is an asethetical judgment, but the judgment of time is a teleology belonging to narrative. Clouds of subjective purposiveness immersed a territory of thought in the ocean of anger in Huey's thigh. He swam forward, thinking about mustard.

His jacket was by now quite obviously wet though a few vagrant birds still adorned its lapels and held secret almonds in their beaks. Santa Claus descended in a balloon and gave everyone a kitchen and a garland of bosomy African volcanoes ripe and plump and ready to spurt. Stallions and sheep exited the casinos holding wads of cash in their mouths.

Sleep was a bulky road of nomadic cattle, a novelist's fight for justice and freedom and a pair of black Brazilian shoes.

As the locomotive heaved out of the lake and pulled out into space, the face of Huey's mask filled with a featureless sky over pale smooth water, where a seagull was hanging with wings fixed, like a violin poised for producing a powerful outflow of experience and goldfish.

It has often been said that the violin is an instrument capable of anything, including empire, though in order to make the instrument sound louder, one must increase the string tension. In order to do this, one must be willing to wear cashmere with a necklace of pedagogical gallstones. Bells take time to ring into wash and tubas shoulder the bulk of juxtaposition, leaving the armpits to spin in indolence like right angles in a laundromat. Huey floated serenely a moment feeling deliberate and dear.

His arms teemed with endeavour. His glands secreted punctuation.

Most of Tahiti, he thought, consists of electricity.

This was correct. All art is quite useless. Feelings, on the other hand, are unequivocally arbitrary.

Feelings of pleasurable sensation can only be established *a posteriori* through the medium of experience itself. A thousand feet in and 130 feet down Huey came upon a garden of life. The bottom was rich with feather duster worms and sea cucumbers. Here the representation is altogether referred to the subject and to its feeling of life, under the name of the feeling of plebiscite or painted lady.

While it is true that everywhere there is wisdom in the making, the violin is a science, not a fiat or some fat Rio Grande of watermelons and salmon.

There are no salmon in the Rio Grande, only marble satellites emitting baroque architecture and rubber generators of floating visceral champagne. To think otherwise is to delude oneself into believing the Mississippi is a river, instead of a cello.

My armor of snow, my coral kilohertz, my immense neglected floor, thought Huey, are all wrongly engineered and flagrantly burlap. I feel truly ermine. I feel the bones of my spine turn cold as a shirt with no fabric or buttons but only the hours of a sunken bottle trickling patterns of sleep on the braided nomenclature of a woven strip of narrative galloon.

By the time Huey surfaced into disease and disorder again he felt something shift slightly in his throat and parachute through his afternoon sprinkling simplicity and croquet. It

was a sentence, a long sentence of clouds and nerves climax-
ing in telescopic glissando. Huey decided to quit the factory
and become a suffix, a lever at the end of a word he had not
yet coined, but would require another visit to the bottom of
his lake, the big injection of medicine glittering under the
sun like a simile, or smile.

THE MYSTERY OF GROCERY CARTS

I AM SITTING in the car reading Russell Edson. It's raining
heavily. Roberta has gone into the grocery store for whipped
cream and lettuce. The car is parked in a large parking lot.
Water flows down the windshield in blurry sheets through
which I can barely make out the red neon sign across Queen
Anne Avenue North that says Hot Subs Elliott Bay Pizza
Company. A man in a blue shirt gets into a blue Dodge and
drives away. A younger man in a green Volkswagon Rabbit
with a crushed left fender takes his place. A man walks past
with a cigarette dangling from his lower lip and I wonder
how he has managed to keep the cigarette going all this way
in such heavy rain. He is almost finished with it. He stubs it
out and goes into the grocery store. I look to the left and
notice beads of water dripping from the wires of the grocery
cart. Wait a minute. Are they wires or rods? Is there a word
for that particular part of the grocery cart anatomy? Would
they more properly be described as bars? Crosspieces?
Crossbars? Meshwork? Webwork? Reticulum? I suddenly
realize how arbitrary and limited language can be. The
inability to describe the framework of a grocery cart, or the
way the water descends the windshield, or the contrast
between the poplars wavering in front of a gray sky, the
acutely delineated branches of the poplars against the
amorphous gray of the sky, which isn't actually gray, but
more of an opalescent off-white, with here and there deep-
ening areas of gray that diffuse into the white. Perhaps I
could say the sky holds the garrulity of milk in its murmur of
rain and oxygen. The meat of the air sings to the mud of the
earth and as the rain splatters against the glass of the wind-

shield the emotional life of the sky describes itself as a rubber band of deep silence stretching into the galaxies in which the gentle truth of apple blossoms are invented in troughs of promiscuous ambiguity. But none of this solves the true problem at hand which is what to call the rods or wires on the framework of a grocery cart. And when did the grocery cart first enter human history. Did the Sumerians use grocery carts? Did the Babylonians use grocery carts? Is the grocery cart an adjunct of the automobile? Do the nomads of Mauritania long to push grocery carts? Why do so many grocery carts find themselves lying in creeks and culverts and roadside ditches? Where are grocery carts produced? Is there a city known for its production of grocery carts? Is there a Detroit of grocery carts? Roberta returns to the car with whipped cream and lettuce and a bunch of other stuff. "Where to now," I say. "Let's go to the video store," she answers. I start the car and we leave. I say nothing about grocery carts. I decide to leave the mystery of grocery carts alone for a while. My thoughts turn instead to the complexities of driving, and the fathomless mystery of gas, and combustion, and what movie to rent, and the harsh yet wonderful glow of taillights in spring rain.

GRAVE 53

FROM MY SEAT beside Grave 53 I can see a shaded spring offering buoyant relief to a herd of ponderous hippos. The tangled limbs appeared priceless and dead. Somehow, long letters and telephone calls never bridge the gap that touching can.

Some of the graves are shaped like beehives. Others like a Saturday afternoon. A few resemble the thumb and forefinger of a pharmacist I once knew in ancient Sumer.

The summers in Sumer are hot, let me tell you. Each day carries the smell of Ishtar, the kelp beating the shore at the delta of the Tigris. It is a phenomenal place for dinosaur hunting. But walk into the Institute of Mathematics today and you'll notice a catastrophic algorithm spitting pixels at a fractal star. Centuries-old coral has to be removed to get to the sunken gold.

I strode down a long, dark corridor admiring the various trapezoids. Mechanical flickers convince the lions that mud is linked to clouds and this reveals sleep. The halls have been rubbed for years by clavicles of noise. The railroad proclaims elephants and the stallions stand and glare as the camera magnifies our behavior as it is put together with anesthetics and leaves.

Oxygen builds the carrots into hardware. A gnarl of yellow promulgates bones and buffalo.

I entered another wing of the institute and plunged into a different world. In the house of the dead the noise of a fire crackling briskly in the cold air can be heard from a distance. I gripped the safety switch at the back of the gun housing, though what good a .45 was going to do me I couldn't really say. How do you drill a hole through air?

Scorch marks and bright debris indicated the existence of something regal and quite possibly vertical. I tried to make the tiny artificial Christmas tree in my breastpocket mimic the sound of a preposition bouncing through a honeymoon. I felt 14 feet of muscle and scales sweep past my legs and turned cold as a marble hibiscus.

Adrenaline was pumping wildly through me. I was completely lucid, maybe for the first time in my life, but I couldn't fathom why this was happening to me. The future of the trumpet unfolded at the gate of my perception. I tossed a bucket of perforation on it, complete with tinsel and blinking lights, and ran back to my roost at Grave 53. An impending splendor could be seen in the eastern sky and the gaunt, careworn features and dusty figures of the Civil War dead went trooping past.

How many cell phones is a gorilla worth?

It's something I've wondered about for years.

The girl the networks called Supergirl was now a world-wide obsession, and her beauty and powers made her the most sought-after celebrity on the planet. Spurting patterns of coniferous silver adorned the ancient snowshoe of dawn and I could now see how democracy grants totems to some and ideas of coconut to others. How fruit is often idealized as unaffected organs of fecundity and how the antiquity of garlic pulses with the neutrons of the underworld.

I picked some bullets up from the ground and strolled back to my car thinking about dawn and Supergirl, the troughs filled with ravens and my dashboard global as capillaries on a basketball.

Existence is elsewhere, I muttered to myself, and rubbed some condensation from the window. There in the distance sat Grave 53, my grave, your grave, anyone's grave. A grave grave engraved with gravid ambiguity, the fruit of another world, a place full of liquid and salt.

AND DROWSY TINKLNGS LULL
THE DISTANT FOLDS

WHEN WE RIDE in a car we become ghosts, indirect
objects in a racket of trapezoids and string. There is no such
thing as Marxist rope, not unless it has been threaded
through a blister, a radiator of mirrors, like a story by Edgar
Allan Poe. I became a ghost of words the instant I took the
wheel, a cloud of primordial incense churning continually
through the night, attempting to tinkle, like something
mystical, which doesn't belong on the highway anyway. And
so I put it here, shackled to Mont-Saint-Michel, next to a
dollop of literary insolence. I have a blue canoe for sale and
you can take a look at that too, after dipping your body in
the cool water of the very idea of it. The idea of water, which
is pinned to the windpipe of a vacuum somewhere in the
collision shop, next to a blimp, there on somebody's table to
illustrate silver, or the idea of silver. Or can it rather be the
idea of helium, or coherence or reproduction, both of which
are implicit in the folds of the curtain and the convolutions
of clouds partially obscured by the folds of the aforemen-
tioned curtain, or the idea of a curtain, which in this case is
thickened in pleats and implication. So do bright things
come to confusion. Or the idea of confusion, some of which
is absorbed by the sand, and some of which corresponds to
reality, or the idea of reality, which is nothing without
irreality, or the idea of irreality. The clitoris hanging in the
air of all this speculation is more than mere syllables and
salt. There is often an extenuating circumstance that opens a
window on an unexpected latitude, a shower of gold undu-
lating over the waves to the starboard side and coming

closer, so close we can almost smell it now, taste its sparkle and hyperlucidity. Ay, now the plot thickens very much upon us, though perhaps due more to the lighting, than the throng of valves convulsing in conversation. The clitoris is a vector of pleasure, a pound of constant guessing, and sometimes appears in a burst of sound with the speed and force of rapid water crashing over a series of rocks, an invigorating idea of something I shall most likely never experience, except from the vantage point of imagination, a hymeneal differential I have sewn with irrational thread, or the idea of thread, which is dry and momentary, a suggestion of mauve lost among thick pearl gray clouds drifting over eighteenth-century France, or the idea of eighteenth-century France gusting with causality and smells. Not just the idea of causality, but all the slingshots and lint that go into the proposal of something larger than a sentence, larger than the rumble of a thunderhead, or the crunch of gravel. Some-thing like a narrative of water, or amplitude in the form of a plant. Something moist and ineffable. Something like a mimosa, or a billfold full of crumpled dollars and turf.

MATIÈRE CHARBONNEUSE

CLAY TRICKLED from my crutch, although it was obvious
I had no crutch, the crutch was a fiction, a non-entity, an
imagined object, an abstraction. The crutch was an abstrac-
tion, in the way intimacy is sometimes an abstraction. We
allow ourselves to become intimate with the idea of inti-
macy. We may be riding a bus. We may be on our way to
work. We may be casually browsing a newspaper, or reading
it earnestly, so earnestly the paper and ink and photographs
all appear to have an intimate connection with our lives, the
president and vice-president, the secretary of defense, the
secretary of the interior, the secretary of secretaries. Mean-
while the piano grows hair and becomes an animal, an
animal of music, its strings bubbling with animal-like
sounds, pure cardboard sounds, a long dark howl of card-
board. The blood of a terrestrial goldfish is not gold. This is
why I keep a small waterfall in my stove. The further devel-
opment of Lavoisier's views on matiére charbonneuse, plant
and animal substances, and ultimately on respiration, was
enmeshed more tightly than ever within the framework of
his research on the composition of water. So I decided to
join in, to become intimate once again, this time with a
substance, with an element, with the element of water. I
would not recommend too much intimacy with fire, fire
cannot be trusted, sometimes it is our friend, and sometimes
it rages through forests exploding and roaring with unimag-
inable force, force that is hard to imagine, if not altogether
impossible to imagine, unless you are there, fighting it,
becoming intimate with it. Intimacy with water is easy. Jump
in a pool. Take a shower. Take a bath. Personally I prefer

showers. The water bounces off your skin creating a tingly sensation, lightly caressing your muscles, the muscles that become sore, sore with intimacy, intimacy with gravity, and resisting forces. The wobble and sway of the bus as you become intimate with a newspaper. The wobble and sway of the bus as you become intimate with the scenes passing outside. Outside in the rain. Outside in the fog. Ameliorating Europe. Ameliorating Africa. Ameliorating North and South America. Mystical bullets of falling rain, dropping rain, sentences and spirals of rain, bright luminous drops of rain, creating surf, creating form out of chaos, creating chaos out of form, and intimacy out of abstraction.

SOME THINGS I HAVE SAID

THERE ARE some things I have said of which I am not altogether confident. When I said the stones were miniature volcanoes with Kentucky zippers, I meant Tennessee zephyrs. And when I said the sheer joy of despair is worth a room at the Waldorf in New York, I meant the bracelets I am wearing were jails in themselves and that my name rumbled with trees whenever I resolved to submerge our kitchen in a perception of liquid. I did mean, with all sincerity and confidence, that there is a mouth chiseled out of the vapor of the space surrounding the beverage of a religious spine of fluorocarbons and ghosts, but that the image was overcomplicated, and came apart easily, crumbling apart in the hands like oysters, or the trumpets of oysters, which are sparkling incidents of fiction distinct as the wrinkles in your hand. It is true that the dogs of Minneapolis have been puffed into glass, so that when they bark, or scratch themselves, or chase a stick of some sort, oak or maple, or perhaps the broken end of a broom, that the hues within their anatomy tokened heat and candy. I couldn't help but blurt out the truth of flowers. Flowers insert descriptions of themselves into the mouth in such a fashion one cannot help but issue them forth, ventilate them, trickle lightning from the corners of one's mouth as one's very tongue moves up and down, and from side to side, inventing names for their colors and shapes. Blessed is he who carries within himself a gardenia, an ideal of beauty, and obeys it. I really meant that. But when I said my elbows were caverns of ice I meant only that they resemble bowls of disintegrating light, and that when I moved my arms, dollops of Australia fell through my fingers

igniting passionate reds and aboriginal greens, songlines of
such tangy extension they feel archived in a future tense,
morning dew stitched into the bikinis of the clouds. When
you return to the kitchen you should shut your eyes, and try
to imagine the sincerity of almonds, the cleverness of salt
and the glacial indifference of sugar. Try to construct an
empire of statement, of things unsaid and yet aching to be
uttered, so that when your mouth opens and the words
come out, you will mean them as a swimmer means to swim,
as forms curving and carving their way through the waves.
For nobody doubts the sincerity of waves. They swell into
transparency like a grammatical process, the painting of a
rice cake that comes and goes, drifting from garage sale to
garage sale, creating and leaving impressions, waves and
reveries in the mind, various associations having to do with
rice, and cake, and painting and representation. This is what
I mean to say. This is what I meant to say all along. That
there is nothing so pure as a crosswalk in Death Valley, but
only cracked mud, blue sky, a regime of sounds and smells
that swell into proximity and buoy us up, then pass into the
treble of a musician calling out to Ishtar, a pure flame of
divinity burning the meat of the sun into a primal mascara,
or ratification of green.

THE MAN WHOSE EYES
CLUTCHED CHERUBIM

A SPIRIT of exploration makes Botany Bays and crowns, but what is in a face when the hand opens? Nature is an angel whistling like a storm. An environment of rivers surges toward description, and gravel and churches.

One is often confused by facial expression. It is vital to reveal the eyes. All is eternal. Outside of our skulls the profusion of stars is an encore that churns above the steeples, repeating oblivion in waves of kelp and Florentine silks. Fossils and suns and fossil suns drop light in the rain during a perception of rubies. It is gratifying to paint a river. Puerto Rico cries out for lemons. Our chariots are pulled by clay hummingbirds whose throats obey the sepia of a convulsive sanctity. I have rubbed the hides of the buffalo until they slobbered like lightbulbs. Mustard laminates the meat. Human needs emerge from the bread. The traction of the stars ingratiates infinity. We have reverence for liquids and what generally pass for tunnels. There is a sky chained to the tableleg in this sentence can you see it. There is a lake frozen to your eye. It looks heavier than a Sonoran honey. The catalogue of insects opens revealing translucent membranes. And then we realize they are words, not X-rays as we originally thought. Even Socrates had enzymes. Have you ever seen a rhythm vomit circles? Personally I prefer Spain. As you can see, it instigates the sauce of evening and misquotes the sun as a goiter. It looks down upon us, edible and sweet and practical as a brick. But faces can be deceiving. I once saw a man whose eyes were clutching cherubim and whose mouth was a box of insects. How surprised I was

when I discovered the man was a tube of armor ejaculating
metal at the idea of blood.

SOME ASSUMPTIONS OF GAS

WHAT IS space? What is the nature of space? Space is what I have in my mouth, the possibility of getting into a boat to let air and vowels out for a name written in water. And here on earth as it is in heaven space is made of air and air is a gas is blowing is cold is chaos is an animal breathing oxygen. The calamity of berries dangling wobbling a hoop of felicity around the sun. Space extends into space and then bends. It is an ambient sunlight. Is there anything more fascinating than a helicopter? Yes, when the word 'gas' is pronounced I find space hibernating in ink and it is warm it is fugitive it is heavy it is light. It is metal or a jeep bouncing over a hill. Is an umbrella like a paragraph. There is something inherently exciting about space we are free to go anywhere we like it is ubiquitous as dirt incidents of elk. Even the word 'gas' sounds like gas, the sibilant 's' an onomatopoetic hiss, gas leaking from a balloon, air leaking from a tire: *gassss*. When space becomes a substance it is everywhere, everywhere like air, as on a boat when one feels the motion of the water, as long as there is gas in the engine, and we are free to travel, to go from shore to shore. Pierce Brosnan and Michelle Yeoh on a motorcycle racing through Saigon extend a sense of space, the fact of a gas like air on the movie screen, a helicopter tilting its blades in a menacing fashion. When I think of gas I think of space. It does not cease to be space. The light fills the air like water soaks a rag, provided there is sufficient wind down by the river, and things in motion. Soft facts hard facts a seed enclosed by a cut. The origin of the universe hidden in substance. One feels connected to the sky when the air fills the garage. I have decided to insert a river

here, some bop exuberance and pancakes and bacon. An
isosceles triangle or a tingle of quadrilateral morning.
Gasoline, ether, nitrous oxide, indigestion. Gas comes from
the Flemish word for chaos. To move the boat is to discover
gas everywhere manifest as sunlight. And this contributes to
jazz, to a sense of jazz, to a finely drawn line or a dwelling
made of clay. So that when we say gas we are really saying
chaos. When we say we need to stop and get some gas we are
really saying we need to stop and get some chaos. Rivers on
Mars, the scent of oil or grease carried on a breeze, the
Montgolfiers over Paris. We are saying all these things when
we say gas. Let us assume gas. Let us assume gas is something
to inhale. Let us assume gas is something to fill the sail. Let
us say the dock is an object extending into space and that
there is water crashing over rocks, burned metal and warm
rubber, or a scroll or a watch. Let us assume helium in a jar,
quantum rain, a mule in a Mississippi bar. Let us assume gas
is something to exhale like giant floods on Mars. Let us
imagine a word filling space as it was meant to be filled with
the skeletons of sound. Let us construct a balloon of silk, of
vinyl and leather and bubbles and baubles, of iron and tweed
and chrome and glass. Let us assume this because there is no
actual substance there is only space. Space and time. Space
and time feel different from one another but they are the
same thing. Let us assume gas fills our balloon with suffi-
cient hydrogen to lift us into the heavens. And we rise and
rise and the air is without shape as the balloon continues to
bulge. And that to bend space is to bend time and to bend
time is to bend space. Time feels like a cage but not up here,
not in the sky. Not in this gas called air. Below us mesmeriz-
ing patterns of waves in which the water informs us of its
movement. To bend time is to put words in the mouths of

ghosts. Ghosts of ink, ghosts of words with their clacking
bones and clicking pearls. Air is a gas and many French ideas
confirm this. This is the nature of possibility, experiments in
chemistry, a broken sentence leaking images of heaven.
Brilliant deep blue-green emeralds. Vocal chords. A sack of
silk inflated with warm air. With a warm idea. With the
pitch of walnut and the humming of signals. A gumbo rife
with flavor and a grape between the lips.

MAHOGANY

EVERYBODY has thoughts but what are they? It is life out of control, beyond limits. The chiseled rocks and northern lights of the arctic regions. Socks and cupboards, electricity and clay. It is the ability to think of a border. A border is an abstraction, like prepositions. A preposition is an idea of space, of being in relation to space, of being under, over, in, on, or at a workbench. Metal is thick. We know this. We also know that water is sometimes a thin thing, sometimes a thick thing. But can anyone see a thought? Can anyone see the illimitable humid airs freighted with frangipani? A poem of opulence and phantasmagoric splendor might suggest moons in the toes, or toes in the dirt. A circumstance which might only exist on a map. Humidity and heat and soil exist elsewhere, exist in a dream at once thick and thin, like water. If one slaps water with a speeding boat or a pair of water skis the water will feel hard. But suppose the thought of this is put into words, into light flooding over the horizon, or the hold of a ship anchored off the coast of Madagascar. Suppose the ship is mahogany. Then the thought, and the ship, the thought of the ship and the buoyancy of the thought, are all mahogany, although mahogany, a durable but heavy and expensive wood, might be an unlikely wood for a ship. Nevertheless, the mind fills with thoughts of Madagascar. Mahogany and water and orchids and vines. Thoughts of water. Thoughts of vines. Thoughts of Farafangana and morning. And each thought, rigged as it is with rope and daylight, might float a world of sensation called a word. The word 'residual,' for instance, which has something in it like roots, the smell of roots. If roots are the theme of a plant then what are its leaves? Are leaves thoughts? Could one reasonably say I see what the plant is thinking? Or if one draws a picture of mud and humus and vines is there something else, something erotic perhaps, contained in the atmosphere? Why are tropical regions so inherently erotic? It is because everything seethes with life, or jumps into the water from a high place, creating a splash. Coins are a form of thought, mandalas of currency. Insects think in groups. A cloud of insects seething and swarming and teeming in the air suggests thinking is thick and thin simultaneously. It's ultimately all about structure. The sun is a gas, but one cannot put one's hand in it because it's too hot, and far away. The tangled vines of Venezuela ratify the punctuation of butterflies, various modes of pollination involving bees. In this world it is obvious that structure is synonymous with idea, the heat and seething vegetation, the pure golden energy of the sun pouring down. It is life without the cold of winter to forge chains of restraint, strange crystals emanating fabulous luminosities of surreal fable. William Blake said energy is eternal delight and of course he's right. Therefore the sun is a pure delight, a moiling boiling mass of golden energy, nuclear explosions one right after another, music in the form of songs, life at its most savage, the heat and seething competition among orchids and vines, everything leading up to mahogany, the idea of mahogany. A book might contain clouds in the form of words, a dreamlike atmosphere transformed into a weave of cloth, and it is here that the idea of mahogany passes through the fingers like air, or the prickliness of straw making a radio crackle. Imagine mahogany as a thought, an intonation or meaning. A language like meat and eggs, or shirts and shoes, gourds blasted out of the tongue. Rhythm is thought. Timbre is thought. Melody is thought. Harmony is thought. Mahogany is thought. Feasible feathery feelers probing tropical gleams of eyeball bog. Dinosaur fossils just beneath the surface of the jungle floor. Miles Davis shaping a sound. Coleridge writing Kubla Khan. The sun eternally at the center of things shooting veils of golden energy into space.

PHILIP'S BIRDHOUSE

PHILIP ENTERED this birdhouse in our last contest and here it is, bubbling with wind songs like an aromatic casino. A happy blend of thread and biology, it is made of cartilaginous butterfly glass ground to resemble a fold of tissue in California. It is imbued with the scent of vanilla and chuckled in a Franklin stove with a bushel of locomotive breath. What makes it even more special, however, is the way its various arteries carry hemoglobin and Mercator projections among the derby cocoons. Each evening the railroad reinvents itself as Philip goes out and attends to various details, such as the Eduadorian door with Belium bells or the tweezer chandelier hanging from the Malayam dragon wire. Last winter Philip found six Jurassic eggs freshly hatched and steaming in a nest of mycotrophic wildflowers, bastard toadflax and Job's tears. What a rewarding experience it is to commune with spring in a Santa Claus suit, and sit in the shade of an acacia holding the granite intestine of a Welsh jeep on your lap while the door swings back and forth and that old buffalo you pumped out of the radio one night during an electric storm holds itself together with twine, its little arms shaped like crocodiles and its immense green eyes X-raying your kneecap as if it were an experimental stovepipe bursting with sumptuous warmth. Join Philip now as he demonstrates how to build an elephant out of bathrobes. When you are done, why not give it to the birds. They will live in it and raise families. One day you may find a little plump cloud of feathers assuming a pair of wings and opening its mind to suggestions. I generally wear a bush jacket for such occasions, and wander about the backyard

holding a flashlight made of ice and reproductive organs.
Imagine the personal satisfaction you'll feel dragging a
landscape out of your bosom and scouring each anodyne
until it shines. Whatever you do: Don't skimp on equip-
ment! Buy a trisaccharide that's stylish but not too hectic.
Look dry as anger at the sun as it is subdued by night. Notice
that one nipple may be larger than the other. Allow yourself
to harbor some suspicion occasionally. What is the weather
of a thigh, the climate of a foot? Think of the various smells
of paint and clay in the halls of an art building. Words are
invisible but we can see the images they make in our minds.
This will lead to elevations unsullied by the weight of the
earth and struggles to butter the light where the rocks
enlarge with music. When this is accomplished, the rest of
the birdhouse will go together easily, like a girl in her middle
teens tapping brads into a baseboard.

ORACLE BONE

GOLD IS neither the rarest nor the most valuable metal, but it makes a nice sound, and helps buttress an otherwise vague idea of wealth, or the warm finger of an infinite hand. It is also, to some extent, an indication of quartz, or the potential for quartz. Like, say, constructing a fact out of dirt and heat, the way flowers do, dictating fedoras and sepals, filaments and anthers. For instance, why do people chew gum? The flavor only lasts a second. So why keep on chewing? There is something vaguely erotic about it. I suppose because it's a form of nervous displacement, the inner chafing of desire, the murk and music of thick leather and bursting clouds. Blue notes long as moonbeams imbued with salt. As soon as one puts a stick of gum in the mouth the bright luminous colors of tropical fish fill the mouth with the pleasure of floating, a negligent energy delighting in itself, à la rubber, and all that that implies. The places in the shallows where the rays of the sun are broken by the undulations of the water are responsible for a similar kind of sensation. A sentence insulated with commas, perhaps, or the buzz in the vestibule when the mailman arrives. And when he does arrive the poodles bark and the birds scatter. Birds, yes, lots of them, but very few bobolinks or toucans. Where I live I mostly see crows, seagulls, starlings, swallows and robins. Dragons are rare, but they exist. They, too, are a product of sensation: the sensation of chewing, of breathing fire, of flapping a pair of gigantic wings and knocking around in the apartment prickling with tin, fury and inner conflict and some fairly impressive technology developed by NASA. My argument here is that a toolbox is a naked embryo, and its orchestral fabric is beefy, and that when it is picked up or moved things clank around inside. Things like ambition or retribution. The kind of things that inhabit the human ego, which is an egg, a piece of space surrounded by skin, a sequence of protein obedient to the asphalt, the righteousness of asphalt, which must justify itself by forming arteries in the city, and comfort us with lanes and painted curbs. Because there are always places to go but few places to park. Because fluids lengthen into fingers and fingers into rotation. Because there are birds, and words available to describe the birds, and cause them to flutter into bamboo, or occasionally silk. Inscriptions on animal bones emerge during the late Shang Dynasty, serving mostly as a record of divination between a human ruler and the supernatural world. This early incision illustrates the pictographic and sacred origins of Chinese writing. Later we find the speed and informal freedom of cursive script, modulated brush lines with sweeping horizontal strokes ending in sharp tips. A single mark is sufficient to carry the nerves of the mouth into condensations of meaning. Moments of impertinent ink heaved into language like a tree.

CURIOSITY WAS BORN
WITH THE UNIVERSE

Curiositè naquît avec l'universe.
— Le Comte de Lautrèamont

YESTERDAY'S rain led to accordion clouds, freakish testaments of moisture. Today a band of lavender pools in a basin of quadrilateral mint, hinting at endless churning colors regenerating the skin of logic on a glockenspiel.

We invent words to shoot lightning, and this is what we call regret.

What we need is tape and ribbon. Ineffability and plain human concern.

Sometimes I see William Blake riding a pinto into eternity. And sometimes I see a woman's nipple in a universe of elves.

I know it's there. I can hear it when I walk.

Later, when we returned to the VCR, I made the sperm go backward. The chemistry of assault conceives a great black juice of heaving pleasure. As every passion has its proper pulse, the granite balloon of a phenomenal ambiguity rises from a gummed label and pops.

Shards of intellectual endeavor fall to the ground in flames.

The average cow is a perfect example of breath. Incidents of skin and amplitude. Pigment and horn. Cylinders and grass.

Curiosity was born with the universe. Curiosity did not kill the cat. Boredom killed the cat. Curiosity redeems the monotony of the rotor. Curiosity cures fiction. Curiosity fountains the architecture of names.

Curiosity is curious and sneezes morphine. Curiosity is erotic and involves fluids. Curiosity is dreamy as stars, a curiously round sentence of zigzags and quail. Hepatica and autumn. The interior of the sun. The mystery of dirt porcelain and bingo incidents of rail.

The inevitable genitalia of a metropolitan owl.

CAPRICCIO

THE WINDOWS of my poetry are open upon the forests of
the Miocene and in its vitrines shine the languishing rivers of
winter and the chortling brooks of summer.

Listen to the tubas attract the henna of Latin into the
chambers of the Snake River. Listen to the muted trumpet of
Miles Davis lost in a dream of cerise. This is the sound of
obsidian. This is the sound of onyx. This is the sound of a
brain in a skull of feverish opal.

The painter washes himself with the facecloth of the sky.

Everything is stained with color. Even the slow sentence of
conifers is stained with a democracy of green. And women's
hats are thickened by the color of sage in the western hills.

There is no more unity. All the clocks are made of rubber.
The minutes occur as curtains. The hours occur as a form of
lactation, the long slow dribble of time as it oozes from
space. The long slow dribble of time housed in a cabinet of
wood and string. There is no more time. There is no more
money. In the Chamber of the Poem one spoils the marvel-
ous elements of the Big Bang. One takes time and space and
makes a cake out of them. A big cake with the frosting of
angels. An angel food cake. A cake sprinkled with words in a
violent profusion, a garrulous swirl of weather and semantic
anarchy.

At the Boiserie, the construction workers drink mochas
and lattés. All the Saturdays of the world swarm in the heart
like blood cells convulsing with paradise. From time to time
a truck passes by, a long growl of pistons and exhaust and
shifting gears. Sparrows hop around on the patio tables
under the gingko trees. All of this enters into the Chamber of

the Poem and becomes a species of light, a soft green teapot with a cracked glaze. The workers talk. The workers play poker. One of them holds a straight. Another holds four of a kind. One of them mouths tugboat theories. Another cups a handful of shade.

I counsel no one. There is no advice in this poem. This is not even a poem. It is only a poem that thinks it's a poem. It's really just another letter from Vincent Van Gogh. In it, he talks about his preference for mountain chalk (*la craie de la montagne*) over Conté sticks because the mountain chalk is solid and doesn't break apart in the hand when he's doing outdoor sketches. He says the mountain chalk has a soul but that the Conté stick is dead. It is the same with violins. Two violins might look alike but one of them may produce a much more beautiful tonality than the other.

I have long preferred the use of the ballpoint for the construction of letters. Sometimes I use a computer but a ballpoint is better. The ballpoint has a soul. The ballpoint has a soul of ink. Endocrine ink. Smears of existence are rendered in loops and dashes and dots and curves. Smears of existence mingled in endocrine ink.

We are surrounded by letters. If this poem has a message then this is it. We are surrounded by letters.

I read with delight the green of the boxwood shrubs and the pale cream of a rock speckled with black. It is trying to say something about its origin but I am not a geologist and cannot read it. I will have to learn the alphabet of rocks.

Meanwhile I hear the chirp of birds. I cannot hear the wind but I can see it in the agitated limbs of the trees. This is a letter from God. Or whoever writes letters with the air. Maybe it is the wind writing itself. Maybe it is the candy of angels rendered in waves of invisible air. Maybe it is a culmination of thought that has no culmination other than cumulus and convolution.

Everything is a halo. A depth.

The sky is a painting by Cimabue.

Geometry is the candy of philosophy.

This poem is done making statements now you can all go home.

No more statements other than the ocean. The ocean which hangs on the wall like bones. Like flutes. Like nothing ever said before.

The fluidity of thread. The song of the dead.

Black winds untangled in night.

BALL OF LIMBS

HERE IN the noumenal sphere, alligators are parodies, like a
sandwich. We make ourselves happy by talking to secretions
of extraordinary cotton. That prostitute over there is fum-
ing. You'll probably want to go over and say something to
her. Meanwhile, let's pin a few clouds to the sky. All poetry
haunts a tapestry of swifts and tarantulas, a world of mis-
steps and provocations, you cannot get away from it, it's like
demonstrating one's jaws by describing patterns of time,
only to discover time is merely a eucalyptus, a lather of
eyesight penetrated by spikes of preternatural rain. And so
you sit down and ponder the situation anew. You find a
buried treasure in your throat and its gold coins fountain
forth in an arc of powerful narrative, the kind that washes
ashore like kelp at the end of the story with nothing solved
but the missing forceps and the leg-of-mutton sleeves
peppered with hurdy-gurdy warts. It is at times like this I
can hear the stars in your voice. You say: I am a wing chair,
and I believe you, though my belief is a feeling I can't help,
something like the practice of poetry, or breathing, or sex.
We all want to live forever. There is nothing new in that. But
the way the peacocks strut around the parking lot in this
heat belies everything I once thought filled with blood. One
is never alone as long as one is filled with blood. Sometimes
all it takes is a solid mass of sunrise to make the marigolds
bloom into boisterous toccatas. There is nothing arrogant or
disdainful about dawn, nothing cunning or brutal about
blood. One avoids bullets and bulletins and gravitates
toward the gratuitous, where all is fine and noumenal, and
the alligators crawl among the reeds, like words thrashing

around in a pool of sound. I hear somebody's sports car start
and realize it, too, is a form of sentence, an imitation of
nothing but itself imitating itself, not so much a real estate as
an ionosphere, a serious cirrus echoing the secret of the
bedsprings. I feel that a metaphor might come in handy at
this point, a device to convince you everything is real,
everything is either liberating us or burdening us, I'm never
sure which, whether it is up to us to decide or the world.
World, yes, but which world? The one here inside, or the one
out there, the one evolving out of the mist talking about the
movies, all those flickering moments of surface and traction,
car chases and harvests, each word a shell with a meaning
inside, a ball of limbs anonymous as a spinal cord.

DANCING WITH GERTRUDE STEIN

REPTILE haunts.

Linseed to linseed the illusionism is a toolbox.

Strung polynomials.

Swiftly fine so called, swiftly ductile and going all the zeppelin.

Corresponding.

Swiftly fine translucence, swiftly warm theme in eyewash, swiftly warm lightbulb quick thick quickly thickly chronically elongated.

Channeled.

Out made memory quick, out away anthology buoyed, at made gill quick, at spring when.

At was striptease slow at ring stark.

Under was firedog slow, around ground fog day, at grind fog day.

At ground fog and most bawdy.

On a loom, on a loon, on a long loom, at a loom looming large. Loon loom and long suction. At a fat hat that a cat cheddars.

Shudders.

Shatters.

Shutters.

Backyard zigzag and mingle and be thin.

Be take and epic and be deep.

Be elevated and induce and taste zucchini, be shall, be shell, be shall but could would.

Hat that thatch. Hatch that hat. Be shall not feet, be hold yes to temperature, be who arriving in trigger, be trigonometry's pillow.

Twinkle.

Linoleum swimming, shout gimbal, shout theory and weigh canister and pile, pile and scoop, scoop the hoop, hope, hop, a hopeful hopping hoop, small awls, and small awl, all the awls are Ptolemy.

Refract a sky with colossal steam, pages, pages and pages, nine, chronicle, murder the soap, carry hope, carry. Keep wet. Keep watt. Saw a ballad ballast many, arrive with hymns. Arrive with hymns. Arrive and hymn, hymn in, hem. Hem, hymn, hum. Hum the hem. Hem the hymn.

Crinkle each cumulus even this finial and a way to fluff is a haddock, a foaming broth and a corollary cloth, a foaming cartoon and a painted muscularity, a limpid yellow and a just, ever so slow, quarters gushing. Quarters sudden and a lightning drop, thick sleet, thick old onyx collars and cuffs and Yoruba, netted representation, canter brittle, declare a rubber of adjusted bushings and some skulls, some triangle skulls.

Some dancing gravy, some opened carrots, some regular nail permutations, some regular shampoos, some irregular ones too, some such waterfalls, some champion pythons, some bidden faucets, some summer beans, some stitches, some onions, some casinos, some fat brushes, some portfolio chops, some batter and always more, always a galaxy. The butterflies, the butterflies are a parabolic abrupt mirror with sticks with cycads, only with delicacy, only with charm and coagulation and small basilicas and numberless burning spigots to keep the unique and shine, shine this. The tall intrigue which prefigures dignity is other. A superlative beach a genuine impacted venerable sand and oaks and earth and goats and vignettes and lips and voices and feelings and continuing and waxes and angles and atoms and Aristotle and kelp.

Thin warmths and hot envelopes and thick cogwheel
refrain and warmth in the dirty gun and amber pleasing
reason with the fetus in the book and a drool and a tool and
a rare canvas and a blooming wrench and a swimming
luminous moral and a small piece of garlic and a red a red
and a wet red tool and an event and a custard and an enor-
mous consonant and a medium sun gold and a tall wallpaper
breath. A large bronze shape a big piece of cure and a
celebrated genuine pre-Columbian forge and jelly ghost, a
way both anaconda, a way them anaconda thick. A single
dangle is dandy, a dirty raw throat swallowing tincture
ahead. A powder, a dime, a belched knob and a haircut.

ANCHOVIES, YES ANCHOVIES

THE ALPHABET was born in Sumer.

The alphabet was born in clay.

Let us look to the salary of the sun.

The ziggurats are mountains of reverence. The wedges are letters. A muscular thigh exudes the odor of Ishtar.

The anchovie appeared to Ishtar with heat and light and she saw that it was good and kindled the golds and greens of an epic pizza.

The anchovie appears in an image of skin and salt as the word glides from the mouth and the sun strikes the clay of Sumer.

How is it Sumer and anchovies are mingled in the mind?

Mingled like dough. Mingled like smells. Mingled like nudes blowing glass. Mingled like forecasts. Mingled like screws. Mingled like nails. Mingled like the movement of the stars. Mingled like fire and flutes and sticky cognition. Mingled like wicker. Mingled like steel.

I told Randy about the oolitic pudding, the leathers and pedigogical transparencies of the stars of Mesopotamia, and he answered me with sarsaparilla and paint, a thatch modeled on principles of drawing, the lurid vigor of description curling into a liquid reality infringing on the hegemony of television.

And this became a new kind of writing. This became an amity of Gregorian glue and a house of bone. This became drumsticks and Missississippi and correlation. The fingers of a young poet standing at the podium in candlelight, his hand and fingers like a huge flesh-colored spider.

The facts of the air are many dots that comprise the

epidermal blowhole in a pair of Sonoran shoes. Or gazpacho or Madrid. Or the way music curls into cloth and becomes a falcon. Or fellatio. Or thermals of reverie. Or the data of inertia rendered in silver. Or needlework and meat. Various idioms of meat.

Or sediment. Or nervous apology. Or salt.

Or anchovies.

Anchovies.

Anchovies are laminations of meat on the palimpsest of a pizza.

You could say elephants pop out of our mouths, or Sandor Krasna's letters rise to consciousness in wounds of fragrance.

I think of anchovies when those peaceful moments of paint drop through the air as our mouths give birth to shapes of sound.

Language is a junkyard so powerful it seems to overwhelm us at times. Its artifacts bubble into consciousness like a man playing a limestone piano, or Benjamin Franklin being pulled across a lake by a kite. To dig a new entrance to the Mir diamond mine in northern Siberia, workers need felt boots, fur hats, and pneumatic chisels that can hack through 1,400 feet of permafrost. There is, of course, plenty of language on hand to help with this burden. But it is ultimately anchovies that nurture the hungry archaeologists in the skull museum. The hungry archaeologists searching for evidence of other worlds. Other perceptions. Other phenomena.

The idea of time is so big it's invisible.

A crew of humans floating through the infinite à la Captain Kirk and Spock and the S.S. Enterprise.

Disease can be beautiful.

The momentum of water in the mind develops these

sentiments into words. Words full of pistons and explosions and energy.

So do gods emerge from the mind, wounds of salt turning tan and ochre.

Anchovies come alive in the mind with each succulent bite.

It is as if the body were a world of glass and chemicals like the iridescent play of colors in an alembic, maps of a foreign world in which truth is a starry sky on a palette of blades gripped in anger.

When we awake sweating and sit upright staring into the dark it is as if we have blasted through the obscurity of the future into movement and verbs.

Philip suggested growing herbs.

We will order pizza.

We will order pizza with anchovies.

We will move forward believing in invisible patterns. Canyons and gullies. The heat of high emotion. The facts of the air encased in tenses. The severity of the weather. Sperm when the sky feels huge. The joy of anchovies.

The joy of anchovies.

The salty taste of anchovies.

Anchovies on pizza.

Anchovies when the day is long and anchovies for Hamlet's promontories.

Anchovies and slippery coils of thought.

Anchovies and a poem floating the thunder of paint.

Anchovies on Thursday. Anchovies on Saturday.

Anchovies expanded into spheres of odor at the edge of the universe. Anchovies painted by Piet Mondrian with geometrical squares of empirical salt. Anchovies at the bottom anchovies at the top. Anchovies tickled into being anchovies from head to toe.

Anchovies with salami and Canadian bacon.
Anchovies with cheese and pepperoni.
Anchovies awakened in the mouth like Egypt.

MORNING ARRIVAL

I FEEL a devotion to the story, to the divulgence of faucets and neutrons, the train of sunrise and mathematical milk. The train of ruggedness brooding in the metals of history. The train of snow with its blobs of light and problems of consciousness. Its unwieldy flowers humped with beauty. Its entanglements and shoes. Its nostalgia for childhood. Its chug and decorations. Its oils. Its sparkling ideas of napkins and narcotic remembrances of mint. The train of surmise the train of going deep underground. The train full of left arms and blades of perception. The train of glass smashed into premonition. The train of consonants. The train of curtains the train of dreams the train of rebukes and washing machines. The train of pianos and conceptions of mink. The train of nesting in the stratosphere. The train of almanacs aroused by infinite shanks of present tense talking to the wind with a mouth of fire.

There is a sound attached to the word 'curtain' that causes it to guarantee mahogany. Everyone on the train knows this. Everyone on the train feels rustic. Everyone on the train is snapping a picture. Everyone on the train is a pure invention of taffeta and ore. Everyone on the train is built out of water. Everyone on the train is sleeping among facts of scallop and volume. Everyone is a prodigal wonder. Everyone invokes the luscious architecture of fog piping a radical disease of eyes to the lurid resolution of an orange. The orange is an incalculable assessment of juice. The orange is buckled to the humidity of an utterance ripening in hawthorn. The orange is a symbol of beauty. The orange is socially constructed. The orange is peeled and ready for the garbage. The orange

orange. The marvelous orange. The orange aboard the train. The orange train. The train of oranges. The train of a single orange of polychromatic temperature. The orange on its way to Boise. The orange on its way to Kennewick. The orange on its way to Massapequa. The orange in its lantern of prose. The orange in its hypoteneuse of sexual juice.

Below us a river curves into a bruise of iridescent blue. An impertinent plausibility of time plumps itself into a translucent artifact of space. Auxiliaries of verbal undulation pull the train into the chill of morning. The train arrives. The train is arriving. The train is arriving in constellations of bulk and compression. Here is the train. There is the train. This is the train. This is an orange. This is an orange and this is a train. The caribou are gratuitous. The caribou are soft as the present tense of a pork chop. The caribou are unfolding from the day like a hill. The caribou are giving you an image of caribou. The pitch of space in a bulb of volume. The apoplectic assumption of a fish bouncing down the street.

EXISTENCE

EXISTENCE is ceremony: unison, streams of hair, banners in the wind, clashing swords and fireworks, a green current of birds dry as a photograph of lightning. Existence is anything you say it is. If you say electrocardiogram existence is an electrocardiogram. If you say English existence is English. If you say Tagalog existence is Tagalog.

I once knew a man named Fulcrum whose acrimony was pungent and smooth. His brain was full of liquid and his eyes were full of himself. He had a place and time for everything and he often said existence is a wall of valves opening and closing, a facility of concrete and terra cotta angels, reptiles and revolutions. He married a fat insect and surrendered to a rational necessity called sex. Existence is sex, he said, a traction of the air.

Existence is elsewhere said André Breton. Glass poets with glass words rubbing themselves on a road to chaos. As a violin bow scrapes music out of catgut, existence ripples with telephones and text. Exploration requires curiosity. Existence requires thatch. An avowal of balance. A moon moored to the leg of a table on which a sonnet rattles with indemnity and neon and a budgerigar mimics a velvet penis. Languor in a country of speckles and breasts. The waters of a valentine ceaseless as the soup of history creating thought out of light and music out of bones.

Each human head ejaculates thoughts of existence packaged in emotions of phantasmal orange. Consonants and vowels occur as bottles of orchidaceous sound, the pentameter of fish, bluebells of rectification. Much of our behavior is shaped like anchors streaming with the fresh foam of foreign harbors. Each perception spurts avowals of pomegranate and rubber. Each perception is a cage of paradise.

Paradise is dangerous. In paradise, existence becomes a salad of swirling balls and sparkling constellations. Profligacy and vapor pegged to the lips of a California heartache. Aerators and irises. The lingering perfume of death. Gurgling examples of Brazil. The grammar of sugar. The sugar of grammar. The drapery of infinity gently ruffled by the breath of an angel.

When existence insinuates itself into hats and shins we say it is blessed and shiny. Junkyards along the highway into Salt Lake grasp the velvet momentum of a September afternoon. Each crumple, each bent bumper, each hammered grill, each mirror and artery reflect the profligate coagulation of a hemorrhaging star we call a sun. The furious waters of a man's thoughts tremble with the awareness of coconut and bubble into cloth. Existence is the obverse of non-existence. Existence is the fruit swollen with meaning in a maelstrom of words, a nipple of delirious ink.

THE BROOD

SOME of my feelings were rubbed into lamps, boxes of
water one could easily mistake for an aquarium, were it not
for the zithers blazing in a tincture of certitude, the many
dirigibles dripping with vapor and ink.

A few iridescent secrets emerged into rubber, like milk
glands and nipples. I did not, at first, understand the appeal
of this, and then when I saw the possibilities for elevation
and play looking back at me from the mirror, I formed a
square and impregnated the kilovolts of asparagus with the
science of swords.

A deeper philosophy than personality tolerates spring like
an armadillo.

But what did Hegel mean when he said that consciousness
is (1) Sensuous; (2) Perceiving; (3) Understanding? Did he
not mean (1) Eery; (2) Chambered; (3) Accidental. Say we
see a silver BMW parked in front of a boarded up Denny's.
Does that mean (1) Death is scoured with wind; (2) A word
may digest itself in order to produce a fiber of meaning
capable of stretching from the lamp to the coffee table; (3)
the Pomegranate is a Panoply of Texture and Prodigality.

Can I say connotation is silver and denotation is
Carribbean? That connotation is silk and denotation is dirt?

An emotion stitched together with words will distort
every part of speech into a ukulele of crickets and grass. An
emotion is a compound of some proposition to which the
subject assents to curdle into cheese or jewels. This is why its
expression in language croaks with amphibious ambiguity.
The shore is more than an extension of land into open water;
it is a junkyard for the eyes; it is a place where our eyes,

which have grown tired of things pertaining to land, can be released from their bondage to bushes and bushels, highways and pianos, personalities and outbursts, photographs and government and find truth in the gentle arrangement of shoes.

Each city stimulates visions of water. There is no river hanging in the closet that does not in some way enjoy the vagrancy of its folds, the harmony of its sleeves. The Volga fills the room with odors of Russian fur. The Mississippi hangs tensed with tendons of evident music. The Yukon hangs in a museum of ice. The Seine is a phrase fugitive as a memory of air, the Parisian rain dimpling on its surface.

Think of a word as a decanter of wonder smoking with battle, the cartilage of a turtle crawling in the sand bubbling and stinking of food. Rub that emotion with a brain, and what you have is savor, an interlocking brood.

THINGS TO DO WHILE
WAITING FOR THE BUS

DEMOLISH the core of the global wax of mishap shake the fig for its gamut of hazes squish the bone of turgidity clash with the colors of isolation smash the secret hibiscus disrupt the velvet optimism of knowledge stretch the rubber band of contradiction shiver like a foxglove in Kentucky squash the refrigerated silence of complacency with the apple-jack beats of exigency pop the balloons of demagoguery teach the peach the deckle-edged extensions of juice in a pickle topple the fat pattern of crisis beat the electrical thickets crumple the pharoah's structure bang the waterfall into warmth tumble through life singing adventures of skin disentangle the ganglia of proximity bruise the hydropower of pepper clobber the machine of rhetoric with prayer collapse the meaning of light into utterance.

Never hit a youth whose cargo is made of music. Never sit down on a cat. Never say never. Never mix coffee with steamed parakeets.

Hit the villains of subsidy with the museums of velocity. Wreck the ancient Gibraltor toupee chip the spinning mystical plate shoot the tube of life in your metaphysical bones punch the irises into goats break the trophoblastic fruit into exceptional forces crush the exotic bewilderment of gravy with the propulsion of Egypt shoot the junkyard cattle with 50 meters of kindness and a carpet of moss wrestle the tetrahedral gas into plainsong and sweat decimate the panatela pancake until it regenerates green crash through the light until it scatters into the nerves making angels of us all kill the circumvolution of merchants with the

corrugations of elegy burst out of the cathodes of illusion
mingling bracelets and knobs.

Smear the conspicuous etiquette of death with turmoil
and pharmacies of lavender vocabulary dent the dry society
of men with the decongestants of women shatter the cham-
pagne into a thousand Doric dots build a camera out of a
shoebox and a bone blast the plateau of cylinders into pints
of effulgent reason plant a star on a lithium rhododendron
smudge the bundles of palpable lingering with the oils of
ethereal routine ribbon paradise with rhubarb collapse the
prelude of a dog into the aftermath of a heron hunt for
obsidian pipes clap Europe in jail spatter the fens with rue
and cartwheels splinter the heartache into glass spray what-
ever yellow is necessary sting the sword with acres of stab
mangle the blaze with radically viable outrage crack the
bikini into rumba speckle the head with liquid genesis
wallop the pepper with salt spout truce with the sticks of
friction precipitate tweezers inflate the lullaby of surface
with the epiphany of a Saturday afternoon.

THE REVOLUTION OF LIGHT

THE REVOLUTION of light will occur at night. The revolution of light will bring definition to cassettes of linoleum and symphonic Rilke.

Propellers will turn in brilliant hardware.

Binomials will harden into jukeboxes and carpentry and bone.

Clutches will be cured by amber.

Coaches will arrive for the transport of silks.

Haddock will mature in seas of shivering reality and philosophy and rock.

Books will be written in bright atmospheres of gorgeous epistemological ebony.

Adjectives will blossom in sulfur and sticky cognition. The colors will arouse iridescences of starry precessional swirling.

A swollen sun will flame forth into vanilla and Ferris Wheels of laughing hysterical angles coated with meaning.

Words will inflate with the delinquent grammar of supernatural caribou.

Locomotives of jello and wobbly trinkets of latitude and fruit will deluge the world with rags and rapids and clarity.

The kingdom of death will be made of ice and the cartilage of trout and the railroad will be run by tiny insects. The paragraphs of the living will be linked by evergreens and when the mountains burst into song birds will be birds and horses will be horses.

Soap will float a market of wickerwork and clean wonderful hands and spoons and suds and uncontrollable bubbles and superfluous adjectives and Tuesday and detergents and scabs and wetness and the rapture of wetness and buttons and glockenspiels and symptomatic elbow grease.

Façades will burst into clouds and clouds will burst into
Ellen Burstyn and Ellen Burstyn will burst into villages of
burgundy and burgundy will burst into sticks and residues
will burst into willow and willow will wallow in rosettes of
zinc and burlap.

Onyx will be excused from the blues. Linseed will be
liberated from lotion. Cartoons will profit from linen. All the
lights of the universe will flow into parliaments of gloom
and rupture into wild examples of conviction and porphyry.

All revolutions will cease. This revolution will cease.
Ceasing will cease. Gingkos will seize the sun and turn it into
roots and oxygen. Buckets of light and saucers of night.
Objectivism translucence and Dutch. Veins of sight dramas
of bright. Glove compartments resonance and lightning.
Bullets of carnival grain. Rural stockings. Bumps and
mammals. Dreams. Denotation connotation and logarithms
and bells.

A BIG NOISE

LET'S MAKE a great big noise. Everything is boiling, spark-ling, splattering and bright. Everything is henna. Everything is marble. Everything is the name of a cat or the name of a city or the name of a decade.

Life flowers into rhythm at the window of drums.

The song of the prepositions melts in my mouth. At, on, under, around, in, out, from, about. All melt into one large mass of prepositional pudding. All spatial reference tastes suddenly of tapioca.

I ripen into a lamp of Sumerian oil.

I tumble into the street translucent and lavish, a ball of veins.

This is not a joke. I'm not kidding. I mean it.

An angel bounces me to Tacoma. I become a railroad engineer. I write poems at the head of the train all the way to Los Angeles.

And in the morning I open my eyes.

I see a mouth of gold vomiting reeds and shadows.

I see a British heartache moaning like a hatchery of bells.

I see a cat sobbing radios.

I see a mind revel in glue.

I see a museum of ice melt into shoulders and the wild anatomy of laundry.

I believe, as did the Blackfeet and Crow, that thunder and wind are caused by the flapping of a giant bird that lives in the mountains.

Give me rhythm.

Give me temperature and arteries.

Give me a sound that incorporates cloth.

Give me a liquid sound that crowns the intuition of irises.

Give me the hot dry noise of an armadillo's dream.

There is a description of the landscape I like very much as it supplements our knowledge of plants and canals.

The delicious vertigo of foreign cities. Bratislava. Chang-chun.

It is the poet's responsibility, among other things, to tend to the animals. To feed them. To help them propagate. The houses are turned upside down by enormous birds. The poet must encourage this. The women are too well dressed.

The man who sawed himself in half gave new life to the print wheel.

Rhymes and measures obscure the ores of Equador.

Rhymes and measures dim the lights of Rangoon.

Praise be to a woman's hips.

Magic is the engine of youth.

The lumber of heaven is the fortification of old age.

Moo goo gai pan.

The moon is sifted through the breath and issues from a ring of lips.

THE WHOLE HOLE AND
NOTHING BUT THE HOLE

THE HOLE tasted of fallen leather and elicited sensations of pegged Caribbean humidity, a moisture nailed to a cloud of steam.

The whole hole absorbed its meaning from an aromatic Rio Grande, a mammoth truth sparkling among the pages of a book of clay. Fugitive sensations of Flagstaff boomed in the fire.

What, precisely, is a hole? A hole is the behavior of a void mellowed on the floor of a Kentucky shed. A hole is empty of the logic of brass.

All human beings have a variety of holes. This is an essential and fascinating aspect of human anatomy. The mouth is the biggest hole, followed by the anus.

A gun has a hole at the end of the barrel. It obeys the logic of fire.

The diagonal kindles a geometry of funnels and clover. The air is a religious waterfall. It is full of holes. You can see them when the plants chatter with rain.

Crocodiles merge with the thread of the clouds as they drift through the caboose. The caboose is a hole of quiet blood. The stove makes the creaking sounds of a ship when the front left burner is on low. This is because it has no holes. It is a ring of chrome.

Meat mingling with tone sobers the plump woman in her summer dress. This is called the Hole Designed To Shed Water, or the Torsion Of Being In Another Elemental Hole.

The ermine batteries of the ravenous fog propel the interlocking barbicels of the wings of an Intellectual Hole.

The Hole of the Intellect is a timbre of coral pickled in memory, somewhat like a gentle bar of Ecuadorian soap.

The seeds of the Hole of Trajectory is a soft dry noise, like the Pacific ruffled with wind, or a candy bracelet wrapped in burlap.

The Hole of Autonomy is a thermometer of mud registering non-existent temperatures. The apprehension of chickens exemplifies this moment as it divides into fish, demolishing the disease of optimism with exponents of unrehearsed foam.

My thumb and forefinger can feel the consistency of a hole by slowly expanding into a terrestrial mollification of Ishtar.

Most of the weight of ordinary matter is actually the energy of nothing, observes K.C. Cole, who wrote a book about a hole, called *The Hole in the Universe*, which is constructed of words, which are full of o's, which are full of holes.

In electronics, a vacant energy state that is manifested as a charge defect in a crystalline solid is called a hole and in the majestic game of golf it is a small pit lined with a cup into which the ball must be hit.

The hole of the lumber of heaven is pegged to the ribs of oblivion.

Be it ever so humble there is no place like a hole.

THE GOLDEN MEAN

DNA is a molecule. It is a double helix, a ladder twisted in the shape of a spiral.

Why a spiral? The spiral is magnificent.

The spiral is an abstract idea given movement and pollen.

All energy moves in spirals.

Spirals find resolution in spirals.

When plants convey fluid through long continuous tubes the internal strengthening is formed by a combination of broken spirals and rings, exactly as in the windpipe of the dugong.

Let us praise the windpipe of the dugong.

Let us praise tubes and fluid and volute and volume.

The spiral is the windpipe of volume.

The spiral moves fluidly through volume, like the fugue in the overture to *The Magic Flute*. Like the jewel-studded stem of the sceptre of the city of London. Like the five-coiled gold torque of Glamorganshire. Lefthanded batsmen who bowl righthanded. The hair of Da Vinci's Leda arranged like an ammonite. The Archimedean screw. A pair of hands cupped to catch the rain, music illumined on a piano.

All energy moves in spirals.

Spirals find resolution in spirals.

The conical bones of the okapi's horns taper to a glorious conclusion. Plants twist clockwise to follow the sun. The jubilant curlicues of the yellow spadix of the flamingo flower mimic the music of the baroque and the spirals of the flight of fruits and seeds. The logarithmic curves of a Mesozoic Nautilus, or the sparkle of Mozart's sonatas in which the underlying harmonies of nature are given sound and movement.

The apical, middle, and basal turns of the cochlea of the human ear convey the music to the nerves in volutes and murmurs of cartilaginous beauty.

In the first movement of Mozart's *Sonata No. 1 in C Major* the exposition and recapitulation and development consist of 38 and 62 measures, which is a perfect division according to the Golden Mean.

The Golden Mean or Golden Section or Golden Ratio is a Golden Radio of irrational numbers in an infinite progression of whelks and violins.

Mozart created divine divisions in his piano sonatas making the interplay shine into music. Forces working from within against forces and pressures from without.

All energy moves in spirals. Spirals find resolution in spirals.

Spirals comprise an archetypal alphabet, the eternal blueprint for chrysanthemums and cats, persimmons and panthers. Galaxies and embryos create spirals, form patterns of moving energy into whorls and curls and twirls of brass and bronze and gold, the rapid growth of cells on one aspect rather than on the other, which makes a curve in the shoot, and rotates it, as the growth of antlers alters the altar of alternative antler.

The give and take in biological geometry replicates the replicational structure of heredity. So you see the resolution of tension begins with a spin. With the dorsal valve of a Devonian lamp-shell.

The morphology of pine cones and starfish crowns the morphology of music. The morphology of the sonata parallels the morphology of the pine cone in the interrelation of its sections, which depend for their effect on the strength and clarity of the basic scheme, of cone or tone or symmetry or bone.

Forces working from within against forces and pressures from without. This is the music of life. The waxing and waning of energy patterns characterized in the inter-woven ropes and intricate knotwork of Celtic art. A slow balloon of amino acids linked together to form a chain, a protein, or hydrogen bond. A whorl of leaves in a Roman coliseum. The spirals of a Viking dragon, or the Tree of Life, or alternating phosphate and pyramidine compounds.

The spirally folded petals of a ranunculus.

Whorls and spirals on the prow of a Maori war canoe.

The spirals tattooed on a Maori's face are there to confuse the devil.

Medieval monks used to say their prayers within a maze, in order to escape the pursuit of the Evil One.

There is torsion in the fuchsia and torsion in the rock rose. Torsion in the twists of the lobelia and torsion in the coils of the clematis.

The lateral shoots in the blue gum eucalyptus twist into pendulous leaves of ancestral pattern.

Forces working from within against forces and pressures from without. A music hot with the golden ratio.

A clavicle holds the shoulders as a bell holds sound and as a gene holds a pattern of being in a double spiral of spiraling rungs.

At Chambord, in Touraine, there is a spiral staircase containing two spirals, one within the other, so arranged that a man may ascend from the bottom, while the lady is tripping downwards from the top; yet they will never meet or see each other, though their steps and voices are perfectly audible.

The spiral staircase in the Loretto Chapel of Santa Fe plummets up and floats eternally down. It has no nails and no visible supports. It moves up and down like a sonata of wood, a sonata of pegs and nails. It celebrates space like a colossal DNA double helix on the verge of dividing into song.

The sisters of the Loretto Chapel made a novena to St. Joseph and on the ninth and final day of prayer a man showed up with a donkey and a load of tools and built a spiral staircase that hovered in the air like a vision. And then he disappeared back into the New Mexican desert.

Spirals find resolution in spirals.

Torsion in gorse, and the calligraphy of the heart.

ALPHABET SOUP

THE LANGUAGE of the gene is an idiom of soup. It is a syntax of ooze and adaptation. It is a broth of spirals. It is an alphabet of meat.

The genetic language has an alphabet of 4 letters. A, G, C and T. Adenine, guanine, cytosine and thymine. Four letters with 64 permutational possibilities. Four letters for creating gorillas and egrets and barracudas. Four chemicals for creating lilacs and caribou.

Imagine sunlight on a puddle of algal goop. Imagine this algal goop shaping 141 amino acids into a red blood protein.

Imagine protein.

Imagine goop.

The imagination you're using to imagine the protein and goop was once protein and goop. Is still largely protein and goop.

This is about protein.

This is about goop.

Bright luminous veins of startling light veining the methane of the primordial atmosphere, chemicals stirred by lightning into huge Proustian sentences and furious velvet leaves.

If DNA is a ladder, then the nucleotide is a rung. It is the rung that contains the code for replicating itself into a camel or octopus, leopard or baritone.

It is the number of rungs in the ladder, the number of hips in a tango, the number of orchids in a jungle that determines what the twisting, turning, tangled chain of amino acids are going to produce. The sequencing of parts determines the whole, as syntax determines the flavor of a sentence, or the universal rhythms governing plant growth determine the shape of a leaf or the coil of a tendril, as clavicles determine clavichords and clavichords determine touch, as keys determine locks and locks determine keys. As walks determine fugues and fugues determine walks.

It is the order of the amino acids that make up the rungs, that make a warm autumn burning patterns of gold in the leaves, a woman bundled in wool getting into a cab in New York.

The sequencing of proteins produces silk and decorum, fractal objects, cartilage and orchids.

DNA makes another cell by dividing into convictions and friends, Fibonacci spiral pairs, and theories and signatures.

The molecule is a long and irregularly arranged sequence of amino acids, like an irregularly arranged string of colored beads, tree roots, tributaries, lightning. Conspicuous tendrils travel into renown and bells and wrists. Chromosomes shorten and thicken into bighorn and blondes, primrose and woodsmen, magnets and currency. An enzyme then completes the synthesis of the complementary strands in a ceremony of violent consonance and brutal harmony.

Various enzymes are used to unlock and unwind the double helix, so that thresholds of new being may be crossed, so that DNA fragments may combine to produce thrashed water in a hatchery, fins and scales and the geometry of growth may be renewed and carried into veins on a leaf, echoes in a government hall, the lights and bustle of a Reno casino.

The chromosomes unwind back into invisibility as somewhere in a half-finished aluminum equipment shed spermatazoa swim toward the heavy liquids of fate and living forms.

A single gene is a group of instructions, and in the nonlinear dynamics of chaos a swarm of genes becomes a nomadic flotilla whose coding is carried in the rungs and yardarms of the DNA molecule, the tongues and legs of future generations, the steam of yesterday's rain in the tread of today's tractor, a new intermingling and palette of possibilities.

Nature uses accident and diversity to arrive at shapes with the least resistance to wind and water. Nature incorporates the noble numbers in the public epoxy, a doll within a doll within a doll, twigs and salamanders and lunatic basement phantoms.

Several themes flow through life one of which is passionate and mystical while the other is sticky and lewd.

The DNA molecule divides into kites of lambent destiny, spirals and squawks of seagull joy, chromosomes dangling in the wind, sunlight splashed on a memory of water. Electricity and foosteps unleash the poetry within, okra, papaya, gallons of obsidian hunger and the Fibonacci spiral pairs singing Hey Mr. Tambourine Man.

The precise order of words along the chromosome indicate the order of amino acids making up a particular protein, a muscle or fin, enzyme or sentient being full of testosterone and pulp. The aptitude for geography or augury or convening a parliamentary assembly originates in a molecule inside the nucleus of each cell.

Nerve cells form a fabric called skin, which is a parchment or membrane on which may be written a destiny or wrinkle, mermaid or anchor.

Club cars and Micmac attest to the diversity of protein synthesis, which is a process known as translation. A gene might be translated in a wildly colorful tie selected one day on a trip to Milwaukee, or stamp collecting or golf.

Most values or truths coveted by writing are out of reach of mammals and lizards who are mostly involved in differentiation, like chickens scattered in a barnyard or the furious genetic struggle of a structure in turmoil to communicate a bottle or long bar of soap.

The sympathy of a warm snout might be expressed in the basal layer of epidermis on one's fingers or toes, or an echo stitched to the horn of a mechanical skeleton.

Deoxyribonucleic acid is a direct cab to the destinations and catastrophes of our lives, the velvet of our daily reverie.

Hematopoietic stem cells may have nonredundant roles in the delights bubbling from the personality of my shirt, but who is to know if the molecule of a local impulse flows through my thinking like the levity of a regal autumn afternoon.

Poetry is a universe of enactments. DNA is a universe of spirals.

Each gene is a spiral of proteins forming chains of illimitable association, blood and conversation, eyeballs and valleys. This effect requires direct cell to cell contact among dogs and poplars. The nucleus is a furnace in which a human being emerges like a loaf of brain or screenplay. Every moment yields genes that are differentially expressed, that remain images through the delineation of outlines and the viscera of throats disturbed by words, that leap from being to being by the language of genetics which is a tale of two cities told in cells, which is conveyed in the elegant crystallographic x-ray photographs of Rosalind Franklin, provocative and steaming like a postcard from Hamlet.

The letters of the Roman alphabet let a maelstrom of meaning consent to the flight of cattle in much the same way a passionate protein will unleash a double helix of delirious seeds, torrential neurotransmitters deciphering and filtering the realities of a normal existence in the embryos of fruit flies, or flat stones arranged on the ground somewhere west of Kansas City.

Stromal fibroblasts do not a painted garden make, not without a brush and a complicated boulevard of double-stranded molecules winding themselves around in seemingly endless spirals, each one unzipping itself down the middle to form two separate strands of writing which will join in a recombinant delirium of diphthongs and dugongs and oak. A dollop of daydream on a yellow background of Brazilian rubber trees.

Writing is trying always to find more about the essence of writing, the substance of epoxy and the mystery of personality. Genes initiate this moss with spit and literality. The entire alphabet of the genetic language is simple as a bowl of sparkling vichyssoise, the reality of wilderness in cell fate decisions unzipping and zipping themselves into hips and ribs and ankles and hands, into fins and lips and fascicles of epidermal fiber.

It is stunning how a muslin of future narration might bind to the cytoplasmic domains or an epicure might be born in a malapropism one day in Alabama with a banyan on his knee.

The biology of the umbilical cord is profuse with electro-chemical information and blood. Candlight, bistros, and wax. Bass, piano, and sax.

It takes twenty amino acids to describe the silk of paradise. Chromosomes and sparkling sugars. Four letters. A, G, C, and T. Adenine, cytosine, guanine, and tinsel on a Jetta spiraled around the ski racks.

MY MAP

LET ME tell you about my map, my genetic map: over here is Mount Predilection and over here is Lake Peculiarity. This is the hyperborean flower garden of my great neurotic lilies and my subtle obsessive mosses, my melancholy babies and my electromagnetic begonias.

Here we have a Polynesia of Jingled Personal Wounds and this is an archipelago of Contradictory Ganglia.

Here is an archway embellished with small carvings of extraordinary impulses. Thousands of blocks of stone etched with careless remarks and imprudent gestures await enactment in the Hall of Foolhardy Acts. They've survived air raids, poachers, and Martha Stewart.

This is the Rock of Abnormality. It is burned in a Kiln of Indulgence to produce hydrocarbon and peals of laughter.

This is a gene for brooding and this is a gene for lewd and indecent body hairs. This is a gene for pausing to stare out of a window and this is a gene for enhancing thickets of industrial indolence.

These are my Caverns of Regret and this is my Swamp of Remorse. This is a spiral of chromosomal chamber music and this is a fragment of celebrity DNA going haywire in a Macedonia of kinship roots.

This is my capacity for confusion and this is my genetic code for translating bubbles as they dance on the edge of oblivion.

Here is the Inner Mongolia of my predisposition to seclude myself from the twisted iron of history and this huge expanse of glittering jelly is the Aral Sea of my candy-colored volatility genes.

Here is my aptitude for fruit, my penchant for indirection, my twin blue socks and my ancestral irises, my uncanny knack for getting lost and my acidic disposition toward Florida lemons.

This is my Tropic of Delinquency and this is my Continent of Gross Incontinence. This is the Land of the Ordinary Nose and this is the Land of the Normal Adolescent Fears.

This is my Botswana of Biodiversity and this is a grove of fever trees.

This is a pool of Swedish genes and this is a kaluga sturgeon filled with 400 pounds of caviar.

This is my Cretaceous half century of caterwauling and this is my Mozambique of Big Browsers and High Expectations.

This is a gene for never remembering to buy batteries and this is a gene for bad ideas. This is a gene for going to market and this little gene ran all the way home with a dark parka of molecular relics.

This is a pyramidine and this is a tranquil bay. This is a fertile bottomland and this is a rocky outcrop of empty slabs of fate.

This is a Family Tree and this is a fragile thread of Africa.

This is the Sea of Metamorphosis and this is a barge of Junk DNA.

MY FAVORITE GLAND

A GLAND is an organ that extracts specific substances from the blood and concentrates or alters them for subsequent secretion.

How can anyone not love a gland?

A pool makes swimming genial and Rilke. A gland makes saliva generous and available. A gland makes everything groovy. There is a gland for land and walking on land and zigzags and drama. There is a gland for metaphors and a gland for putting existence before banjos. There is a gland for wounds and a gland for buttes and flutes and drumsticks and warts. There is a gland for digestion and suggestion and translucence and sweat.

A ball of ganglia harvests the sky. A gland surrounds it with wrinkles and sand.

There is a gland in the head and a gland in the hand. There is a gland that incarnates sentiment and makes it Saturday and demonstrable. There is a gland that secretes hormones and a gland that secretes Calypso and Kickapoo and screwdrivers and eggs.

The pituitary gland is a lobed structure, less than half an inch in diameter, that hangs from the floor of the brain by a stalk, the infinidibulum. How can anyone not love a gland that hangs from a stalk called an infinidibulum?

Personally I prefer Spain. The light squirts out of a big ball in the sky making blood and roller skates.

The body is an aggregate of numerous glands.

My favorite gland is the one that triggers estrogen.

My favorite gland is an alphabet provoking the naked holes of Tuesday.

My favorite gland is experience.

My favorite gland is a closet full of cloth and rubber.

To be is an instinct. Not to be is a frost.

Ink is a secretion of writing.

My favortie gland is a preposition. A preposition twists the window into Philadelphia. A preposition secretes technicolor sequences of attitude and bearing. A preposition hangs from the floor of the brain by a stalk called a pronoun.

Flags are glands on poles flapping and flapping and clacking and cloth.

A warm transparent supernatural glass indicates a gland of grammar and verbal construction.

Thank you for reading about glands. Thank you for thinking about glands.

Identity is a product of the gland for hope and chimeras.

Aesthetics continues the gland of muscularity.

The volcano is a gland of fire and molten rock.

The gland of sorrow secretes a mechanical cow.

There is no use in finding out what is in anyone's glands you will find out soon enough that a postage stamp spurts borders.

You will find a floodlight in your mouth secreting illumination. You will find a breath in your words that makes them rumble with gabardine and cycads. You will find a gland in your gingham exemplifying genitalia. You will find a brutal ghost of hair on your head and think it is a memory of syllables.

Semen says see the men.

Semen says cement the men.

Semen says see some women persist in conjugation.

My favorite gland sparkles among the evergreens.

This is the time to say that a government is crisp when it

grants mercury and galleries and hallucinates democracy among the rich.

My favorite gland secretes dimes and diameter and dialogue and iron.

It is the helium of everything.

It is what is knightly.

It is what is intricate and hot with life.

It tastes like sunlight.

A PIECE OF WIND

THE WIND blows seeds from field to field and fills sails until the waves turn white with Sumerian traffic on the Euphrates.

The very light is an engine.

The very light is an alphabet.

Writing began in mud. I cannot emphasize this enough. Writing began in mud. Writing begins in mud.

Riddles, impressed with a reed, are embedded in mud.

The endeavor of the riddle, which is to caress the brain, which is to caress and provoke the brain, is embedded in mud.

Mesopotamia punctures the twilight providing the dark with gallons of trances and traces of cat.

The cat is holy in this part of the world and at this point in time because the cat crawls out of the air and pours itself into rubies and bracelets of Sumerian art.

Hillsides are dolloped from a spoon of morning light.

Convexities occur as vapor. Convexities occur as clouds. The clouds drop water on the plains of Mesopotamia and fill the canals with water.

A cloud in the shape of a bear accumulates in cumulus and foreshadows cookware and science.

Southern Iraq blinks with reeds whose structured tubes spurt Sumerian seed at the amalgamated clay that augurs the river.

The drum percolates with rhythm as the wealth of Egypt crumples into sand.

The flute burns with music in the bureau.

The cargo forgives its excessive bulk.

Rubies dazzle the eyes.

The fish divulge magnetism and rags of aromatic abstraction.

Writing is born in disfigurement.

Writing is born in the disfigurement of mud.

The mud of thanks and dried meat and stars and ears and vaginas and morning.

The mud of storms and rivers and haphazard galaxies and Egypt and sleep. The mud of hunger and rain. The mud of vision. The mud of nerves transporting sensations of the outer world to the brain in its skull of bone and sculptured thought. The mud of fecundity and birds and deltas and weather. The wet beautiful mud of arteries and writing.

Troughs of meaning flourishing in particles of sound.

Reveries of sound and permeation.

Reveries of rivers of sound draped with clouds and squeezed into description. A piece of wind pinned to a tablet of Mesopotamian mud.

EVERY MINUTE OF EVERY DAY

BLOSSOMS are fastened to the trees like teapots.

A shoe requires another shoe.

Each personal satellite is painted with the Everglades and soaked in lightning and scoured for parables.

Our perceptions of light are distilled into rocks and roads and rhythms and markets.

An artery of shadows imbues the narration of water with barges of eschatological baritone.

An aristocracy of citrus perverts the ghosts of paradise into cattle.

A Maori warrior goes to a grocery store to buy detergent on the shore of the other side of existence.

A radically viable tube of tin and aluminum illustrates flight and oxygen.

Each butte and plateau represents the terrain behind the mouth in which liquids are flavored with experience and enlarge into words which enlarge into locomotives which enlarge into seeds which enlarge into spit which enlarge into garlic which enlarge into caravans which enlarge into thought which enlarge into watts which enlarge into ingots of music and are incarnated as magnets.

There is a dry word that vibrates like television and a wet word that wiggles like light.

We are moored to one another like rain.

The delphiniums pump color into their petals and expand the morning into hoses and muskrats, halos and lungs.

Marcel Proust rides in a carriage in Paris.

Anthony Quinn and Keanu Reeves stroll through the mist of a Napa vineyard.

A sentence full of ideas and paint sculptured in conversation with the taste of fish and ferns in the Jurassic flaps and ovulates as water carries it all forward into a museum in Denver.

A thermometer stitched to the word "door" signifies biology and levers.

William Shakespeare broils a flower of coral in a raw sonnet constructed of chiseled squares of fiction.

Two shrouded women kneel in the rubble of Gaza.

The freight of this perception tastes of marble.

Amoeba project television.

Distance dangles from the apartment ceiling like a mobile of rocks and velocity.

A Maori warrior shares fighting techniques with a Manhattan lawyer as the rain falls and clouds drift overhead.

The heart of a man battered with winds and testimony cakes into an ear and listens to the ancient beating of the universe.

Alloys and beautiful gleaming surfaces multiply details into endocrine secretions that improvise themselves into somatic utilities and red clouds and words planted in the air arbitrary and blue.

I am finally elected secretary of the interior of a boiling iron finger.

Hips meliorate the torrential meat of human architecture with prominent needs and delicate beauty.

An epic alligator busy with existence reveals the woods and chickens as an allegory of tunings or book full of gentle thermal diseases.

A house outgrows its windows and becomes a genesis.

A dragon blasts flame at a wriggling shadow of trees called rhetoric.

An emotion about the size of a football rolls forward in an irregular and unkempt manner.

A museum opens its doors to a world of relics.

The momentum of water in the mind proves that the electron is a form of garage.

A pair of lungs evanesce with sumptuous shards of Mozart.

The statuary along the wall succumbs to various disasters in order to calculate the sum of the invisible as it is developed behind the ribs.

Autumn etches eternity on a leaf.

A locomotive bursts into truth vomiting energy like a movie.

The theorem of grumbles is purified of melioration and petrified into a hit song at Times Square.

There is jewelry for the neck and arms and materials for building a chassis that is characteristic of thinking.

The melody of malady is sweet, like all of Mexico.

Virtues and visions provide a redefinition of romance as a milieu of surfaces and depths.

There is a wrench inside the garage that is strong and feeble and tall and glass and decorative and green and here it is now totally steel and full of pistons and explosions and energy.

True perceptions entail sweat and sage and heat and rocks and the elegance of Parisian apartments written in volumes like the wind inside the air or the air inside the wind or a sphere of glass with snow in it.

The contours of fish murmur of other worlds as the soft and beautiful Ophelia floats downstream muscle and bone painting the air of a theatre with the diversity of rust.

A warm secret trickles from a machine called breath.